FIESTA IN AZTLAN

FIESTA IN AZTLAN

ANTHOLOGY of CHICANO POETRY

TONI EMPRINGHAM, Editor

Capra Press
Santa Barbara / 1982

Special thanks to the
National Endowment for the Arts
for their support.

Cover design by Terri Wright.
Illustrations by Armando Vallejo, Director,
La casa de la raza, cultural arts component.

LIBRARY OF CONGRESS CATALOGING IN PUBLICATION DATA

Main entry under title:

Chicano poetry.

I. American poetry—Mexican American authors.
2. American poetry—Pacific States. 3. American
poetry—20th century. I. Empringham, Toni.
PS591.M49C5   811'.5'080868073   80-25891
ISBN 0-88496-164-8

CAPRA PRESS
Post Office Box 2068
Santa Barbara, California 93120

TABLE OF CONTENTS

For my mother

FIESTA IN AZTLAN

INTRODUCTION

We left no teeming shore in Europe, hungry and eager to
reach the New World. We crossed no ocean in an over-
crowded boat, impatient and eager to arrive at Ellis Island
in New York. No Statue of Liberty ever greeted our arrival
in this country, and left us with the notion that the land was
free, even though Mexicans and Indians already lived on it.
We did not kill, rape, and steal under the pretext of Manifest
Destiny and Western Expansion. We did not, in fact, come
to the United States at all. The United States came to us.

Luis Valdez, in his introduction to *Aztlán: An Anthology of Mexican
American Literature,* speaks here of a group of Americans whose
creative voices are still for the most part unheard in our culture to-
day. These are Chicanos, people of indigenous American and His-
panic ancestry, born either in Mexico or north of the Rio Grande and
now living within the territorial boundaries of the United States.
They live in Aztlán, the name given by the Aztecs to their place of
origin, the "land to the north" which they left to found their great
empire near Mexico City. For Chicanos, Aztlán represents this home-
land, both geographically and, more important, spiritually, as Carlos
Cumpian's poem "Cuento" (p. 114) clearly indicates.

Why do Chicanos remain unrepresented in anthologies of American
literature and collections of modern American poetry? It is true that
one of the most immediately apparent features of Chicano poetry
is its creative mixture of English, Spanish, and *Caló*—street language
—and that this feature might present an initial barrier to non-Hispanic
readers. As an aid in overcoming this barrier, I have at times provided
complete translations (these poems are marked by an asterisk before
the title); at others, I have translated only the particular words or

11

phrases whose meanings are not evident in context. In all cases, the poems are presented so that they can first be read as originally written, since the mixture of language is very much a part of the total meaning. Those who have risen to the challenge of reading Joyce, Eliot and Pound will find much less heavy going here; we in the United States are certainly more familiar with Spanish than with Italian, French, or Chinese.

My own interest in Chicano literature began in 1970, when I first read the poetry of Alurista, Abelardo, and Tino Villanueva; when I encountered the collections of writings in *El Espejo* and *We Are Chicanos;* when I saw a film on the farmworkers' movement which contained scenes from the *Actos* of Luis Valdez. But though my introduction to these artistic expressions of Chicano culture came relatively late in my life, the force of their impression was a result of something which until then had resided mostly in my unconscious rather than my conscious mind.

Many of the words in these bilingual works I already knew—the foods, the expressions of endearment and, more frequently, of reproof, I had grown up with. My mother, whose maiden name was Feliz, was born and raised on a ranch in the hills between San Luis Obispo and the California coast, speaking only Spanish until she entered school, as did her mother and her mother's mother (farther back our family's memory does not go, but instinct assures me we have always been here). The ranch is gone now, sold to faceless corporate powers, but I remember visits during my childhood, meeting Tío Tata and Tío Frank, who still lived on the land and walked the ten miles to and from town every month with supplies on their backs. And I remember staying with Tía Rosa and Tía Chuco and Tía Jenny and Tía Nacha, my great-aunts, all widowed now, and Tía Florinda, who had never married, in their small wood-frame house on Marsh Street with a giant fig tree in the back yard. I ate Tía Jenny's tortillas, which were lighter and more tender than my grandmother's (but Nana's, thick and substantial, made with white flour and lard, tasted better with melted butter and brown sugar). I remember, too, my grandmother's *pililis*, sweet, crisp circles of dough, hot and puffy from the deep fat in which they had just been fried; I remember her enormous pans of rice and beans and enchiladas, the heavy odors of chili and onion and *comino* which filled the kitchen, the vague knowledge that this was not "American" food.

And I remember being startled by the remark made by a friend I brought home with me one day—I must have been in the third or fourth grade at the time: "Your mother has an accent." "No she doesn't," I responded immediately, automatically. "My mother was born here, my whole family was born here." But my friend was right, and I became aware of something different about the speech I heard at home: not only the Spanish words occasionally thrown out, mostly as reproof—*mentiras, cochina, fregada, embustera*—but also the pronunciation of English ones. My mother did have an accent. In fact, my grandmother had an even stronger one, and at times she and my mother communicated in words I only half understood.

It is this background that led me to Chicano poetry, but although I was at first attracted only by its bilinguality, its intense specific imagery and straightforward expressions of emotion held and deepened my interest. I began to notice certain subjects that arose again and again in the works of different poets, certain themes which emerged to unify their images and expressions. Thus, the observation by the noted writer and educator Tomás Rivera that *"la casa, el barrio* and *la lucha* [the home, the neighborhood, the struggle] are constant elements in the ritual of Chicano literature"* became the basis for my grouping of the poems presented here. The first section, *La Familia,* shows the strong and lasting influence of home life in Chicano culture, and the love and respect with which children and their elders treat one another. The second, *The Streets of the Barrio,* moves from the home to its immediate surroundings, showing a positive force in the shelter and homogeneity offered by the neighborhood; as Luis Rodríguez says in the quotation which introduces that unit, "there is death and violence here but there is much more life." Finally, *El Mundo* (the world) shows the Chicano in the widest context of all: in his struggle to exist economically, culturally, and spiritually despite forces which persist in categorizing him as an outsider in a predominantly Anglo society. These poems sometimes speak with sad and lonely undertones, but not always; those at the end of the section—for example, Alurista's "ya estufas" and María Saucedo's "Sobre la Liberación de la Mujer"—offer spirited solutions to being denied the so-called American Dream.

---

*"Chicano Literature: Fiesta of the Living," *Books Abroad* 49 (Summer 1975), p. 441.

This is not meant as an exhaustive or comprehensive collection; I wanted to bring together a group of fine, strong poems in order to introduce them to new readers and to keep them alive for old ones. I began assembling these materials while attending a seminar for two-year college teachers sponsored by the National Endowment for the Humanities, and I would like to thank this organization for its financial support during that period. Several people have been of particular help to me in selecting and translating the poems: Stephen Montgomery, Stephen Jama, and especially Margarita Baldenegro Reyes and the members of her family. I would also like to thank Noel Young for understanding the importance of publishing an anthology such as this one. Finally, I thank the poets whose works appear here for inviting us all to their fiesta in Aztlán.

—TONI EMPRINGHAM

LA FAMILIA

LA FAMILIA

"My grandson says he will go to the university and work hard there. I tell him that will be wonderful. Then he tells me that no matter what he learns there, he will still look up to me. I say that is also wonderful—and I pick him up and show him I still have some strength left in my arms. Then I put him down and tell him I had a teacher all my life, even though I had so little schooling: necessity is a demanding teacher. Yes, the boy agrees. Then I boast; it is bad to do, but I can't control myself. *Enseña más la necesidad, que un año de universidad.* How would an Anglo say it? Necessity teaches more than one year of university study? Yes, that is what I say. My wife tells me I should be ashamed of myself, bragging like that, but I want the children to know that their grandfather has a useful life. And they are not bothered by what I say. They clap their hands and say hurrah! And I clap back at them."

ROBERT COLES, The Old Ones of New Mexico

*COMIDA

Uno se come
la luna en la tortilla
Comes frijol
y comes tierra
Comes chile
y comes sol y fuego
Bebes agua
y bebes cielo

—*Victor M. Valle*

FOOD

One eats
the moon in a tortilla
Eat frijoles
and you eat the earth
Eat chile
and you eat sun and fire
Drink water
and you drink sky

My Mother Pieced Quilts

they were just meant as covers
in winters
as weapons
against pounding january winds

but it was just that every morning I awoke to these
october ripened canvases
passed my hand across their cloth faces
and began to wonder how you pieced
all these together
these strips of gentle communion cotton and flannel nightgowns
wedding organdies
dime store velvets

how you shaped patterns square and oblong and round
positioned
balanced
then cemented them
with your thread
a steel needle
a thimble

how the thread darted in and out
galloping along the frayed edges, tucking them in
as you did us at night
oh how you stretched and turned and re-arranged
your michigan spring faded curtain pieces
my father's santa fe work shirt
the summer denims, the tweeds of fall

in the evening you sat at your canvas
—our cracked linoleum floor the drawing board
me lounging on your arm
and you staking out the plan:
whether to put the lilac purple of easter against the red plaid of
    winter-going-
into-spring

whether to mix a yellow with blue and white and paint the
corpus christi noon when my father held your hand
whether to shape a five-point star from the
somber black silk you wore to grandmother's funeral

you were the river current
carrying the roaring notes
forming them into pictures of a little boy reclining
a swallow flying
you were the caravan master at the reins
driving your threaded needle artillery across the mosaic cloth
    bridges
delivering yourself in separate testimonies

oh mother you plunged me sobbing and laughing
into our past
into the river crossing at five
into the spinach fields
into the plainview cotton rows
into tuberculosis wards
into braids and muslin dresses
sewn hard and taut to withstand the thrashings of twenty-five
    years

stretched out they lay
armed/ready/shouting/celebrating

knotted with love
the quilts sing on

—Teresa Palomo Acosta

*La Jefita

When I remember the campos
    Y las noches and the sounds
Of those nights en carpas o
Bagones I remember my jefita's
    Palote
    Clik-clok; clik-clak-clok
    Y su tocesita.

(I swear, she never slept!)

Reluctant awakenings a la media
Noche y la luz prendida,

    PRRRRRRINNNNGGGGGGG!

A noisy chorro missing the
    Basin.

Que horas son, ama?
Es tarde mi hijito. Cover up
Your little brothers,
Y yo con pena but too sleepy,

    Go to bed little mother!

A maternal reply mingled with
The hissing of the hot planchas
Y los frijoles de la hoya
Boiling musically dando segunda
A los ruidos nocturnos and
The snores of the old man

    Lulling sounds y los perros

Ladrando—then the familiar
Hallucinations just before sleep.

    And my jefita was no more.

But by then it was time to get Up!

My old man had a chiflidito
That irritated the world to
Wakefulness.

     Wheeeeeeeeeet!   Wheeeeeeet!

Arriba, cabrones chavalos,
Huevones!

     Y todavia la pinche
     Noche oscura

Y la jefita slapping tortillas.

     Prieta! Help with the lonches!
     Calientale agua a tu 'apa!

(Me la rayo ese! My jefita never slept!)

Y en el fil, pulling her cien
Libras de algoda se sonreis
Mi jefe y decia

That woman—she only complains
in her sleep.

           —José Montoya

MOTHER

When I remember the work camps
  And the nights and the sounds
Of those nights in tents or
Wagons I remember my mother's
  Cane
  Click-clock; click-clack-clock
  And her little cough.

(I swear, she never slept!)

Reluctant awakenings in the middle of the
Night and the light turned on,

  PRRRRRRINNNNGGGGGGG!

A noisy stream missing the
  Basin.

What time is it, Mama?
It's late, my son. Cover up
Your little brothers,
And I with guilt but too sleepy,

  Go to bed little mother!

A maternal reply mingled with
The hissing of the hot iron
And the beans in the pot
Boiling musically seconding
The nocturnal sounds and
The snores of the old man

  Lulling sounds and the dogs

Barking—then the familiar
Hallucinations just before sleep.

And my mother was no more.

But by then it was time to get Up!

My old man had a whistle
That irritated the world to
Wakefulness.

    Wheeeeeeeeeet!   Wheeeeeeet!

Get up, no-good kids,
Lazy ones!

    And still the cursed
    Dark night

And mother slapping tortillas.

    Prieta!* Help with the lunches!
    Hot water for your father!

(I swear, man! My mother never slept!)

And in the fields, pulling her hundred
Pounds of cotton he would smile
My father and say

That woman—she only complains
in her sleep.

---

*Lit. Dark-complexioned, "Blackie"; but used as a term of endearment. Thus a closer translation would be "Sweetheart," "Honey."

Beneath The Shadow Of The Freeway

1.

Across the street—the freeway,
blind worm, wrapping the valley up
from Los Altos to Sal Si Puedes.
I watched it from my porch
unwinding. Every day at dusk
as Grandma watered geraniums
the shadow of the freeway lengthened.

2.

We were a woman family:
Grandma, our innocent Queen;
Mama, the Swift Knight, Fearless Warrior.
Mama wanted to be Princess instead.
I know that. Even now she dreams of taffeta
and foot-high tiaras.

Myself: I could never decide.
So I turned to books, those staunch, upright men.
I became scribe: Translator of Foreign Mail,
interpreting letters from the government, notices
of dissolved marriages and Welfare stipulations.
I paid the bills, did light man-work, fixed faucets,
insured everything
against all leaks.

3.

Before rain I notice seagulls.
They walk in flocks,
cautious across lawns: splayed toes,
indecisive beaks. Grandma says
seagulls mean storm.

In California in the summer,
mockingbirds sing all night.
Grandma says they are singing for their wives
who are nesting. "They don't leave their families
borrachando."

She likes the ways of birds,
respects how they show themselves
for toast and a whistle.

She believes in myths and birds.
She trusts only what she builds
with her hands.

4.

She built her house,
cocky, disheveled carpentry,
after living twenty-five years
with a man who tried to kill her.

Grandma, from the hills of Santa Barbara,
I would open my eyes to see her stir mush
in the morning, her hair in loose braids
tucked close around her head
with a yellow scarf.

Mama said, "It's her own fault,
getting screwed by a man for that long.
Sure as shit wasn't hard."
soft she was, soft

5.

in the night I would hear it
glass bottles shattering the street
words cracked into shrill screams
inside my throat   a cold fear
it entered the house in hard
unsteady steps   stopping at my door
my name   bathrobe   slippers
outside 3am mist heavy
as a breath full of whiskey
stop it   go home   come inside
mama if he comes here again
I'll call the police

inside
a grey kitten   a touchstone
purring beneath the quilts
grandma stitched
from his suits
the patchwork singing
of mockingbirds

6.

"You're too soft . . . always were.
You'll get nothing but shit.
Baby, don't count on nobody."

—a mother's wisdom.
Soft. I haven't changed,
maybe grown more silent, cynical
on the outside.

"O Mama, with what's inside of me
I could wash that all away. I could."

"But Mama, if you're good to them
they'll be good to you back."

Back. The freeway is across the street.
It's summer now. Every night I sleep with a gentle man
to the hymn of mockingbirds,

and in time, I plant geraniums.
I tie up my hair into loose braids,
and trust only what I have built
with my own hands.

—Lorna Dee Cervantes

---

borrachando: getting drunk

Bronchitis: The Rosario Beach House

1.
al amanecer   el monstruo del mar dormía
and the sea would lick at the edge
with flat tongues of mercury   quiet and slow
después de leche con café
y pan con mantequilla   mi abuela and I
would go into the water   antes de los otros
she walked easily in the ocean   caminaba
conmigo en sus brazos   the sound of her large legs
parting the water   the legs that later I see
in the sun with sea salt drying white
on her skin   crusada
con ríos rojos y azules
in her black bathing suit

ella en su gordura   floated in the water
como un globo o una ballena   I liked
her way without fear   no como mi mamá
who has always feared water in such abundance
the bath water, no   ni la de lavar las ropas
en el patio   but the ocean, yes
that was one thing out of her influence
but over the sand bars   caminaba
su madre   carrying me
to where seemed to be the end of the ocean
my arms around her neck
sometimes the water would reach my back
a veces más baja but always warm
and so clear   que mirando para abajo
I could see the strong feet of mi abuela
on the white sand   firmes
en agua como si en la tierra

2.

the middle part of the day
I spent con los niños de los vecinos
or others who came to visit   el día
siempre era pasado en chores
y chancletas de goma   running
after the mercocha vendor
who passed dressed in white for the heat
with those long, pointed candies
the color of azucar quemada
or following a straight line
along the water until we reached
la parte mas remota de la playa
more sand than houses
las casas misteriosas
we imagined that brujas or locos
lived in them
out here   so far

3.

la regularidad de esos días
was broken once a week   when mi tío Guicho
would come to take me   a la ciudad
para mis injecciones   in his '46 dust covered
chevrolet that was really black underneath
por el camino pasabamos fincas
fields cupping water   I didn't understand
mi tío Guicho would say: es bueno para el arroz
arroz
arroz
erre con erre cigarro
erre con erre barril
rápido corren los carros
por la linea del ferrocarril
I chanted quietly until we reached the clinic
where I extended the same arm each time

al regresar   muchas millas de la playa
I would stick my head out the window

I knew I was the one who could
smell it farthest away
yo decía: puedo oler el mar

there were three long folds of skin
on either side of his mouth
when mi tío Guicho laughed

4.
por la tarde
nosotros y los vecinos   would drift
out of our houses to fish
todos nos sentábamos a la orilla
on large barnacled posts nailed to the edge
with ladders reaching to the water
our padres or abuelos   smoking
their tabacos to one side of their mouths

la gradual caída del sol
made us swallow our words
as if we were the ones swallowing the sun
aveces uno o otro gritaba   feeling
the rod slip in his hand
los niños corríamos a ver
to see the media luna that had been caught
always the same   all of them with eyes that never closed
without speaking   nosotros, los niños
would draw out feet from the water
as long rectangles of light stretched
from the houses across the gravel road
and to our backs   we knew
that water could swallow you
into nightmares now   it was the place
out of where night rose and was absorbed
into the air   era la hora
cuando no se podía confiar en el mar
o en las cosas familiares del día

we made the world smaller
and brought it inside in our buckets
with the blue and silver fish
we fried in manteca
until the eyes turned white
like the nieve we had never seen

5.
the house trembled with my coughs
y los respiros de mis fantasmas de noche

—Aleida Rodríguez

EXPLORATIONS
BRONCHITIS: THE ROSARIO BEACH HOUSE

1.
at dawn   the sea monster slept
and the sea would lick at the edge
with flat tongues of mercury   quiet and slow
after milk with coffee
and bread with butter   my grandmother and I
would go into the water   before the others
she walked easily in the ocean   she walked
with me in her arms   the sound of her large legs
parting the water   the legs that later I see
in the sun with sea salt drying white
on her skin   crossed
with red and blue rivers
in her black bathing suit

she in her stoutness   floated in the water
like a balloon or a whale   I liked
her way without fear   not like my mother
who has always feared water in such abundance
the bath water, no   nor that used for washing clothes
in the courtyard   but the ocean, yes
that was one thing out of her influence
but over the sand bars   she walked
her mother   carrying me
to where seemed to be the end of the ocean
my arms around her neck
sometimes the water would reach my back
sometimes lower down but always warm
and so clear   that looking from below
I could see the strong feet of my grandmother
on the white sand   as firm
in the water as if on dry land

2.
the middle part of the day
I spent with the neighbors' children
or others who came to visit   the day
always was spent in shorts
and rubber sandals   running
after the candy vendor
who passed dressed in white for the heat
with those long, pointed candies
the color of burnt sugar
or following a straight line
along the water until we reached
the remotest part of the beach
more sand than houses
the mysterious houses
we imagined that witches or crazy people
lived in them
out here   so far

3.
the regularity of those days
was broken once a week   when my Uncle Guicho
would come to take me   to the city
for my injections   in his '46 dust covered
chevrolet that was really black underneath
on the road we passed farms
fields cupping water   I didn't understand
my Uncle Guicho would say: it's good for the rice
rice
rice
double *r* cigar
double *r* barrel
rapidly run the cars
along the railroad line
I chanted quietly until we reached the clinic
where I extended the same arm each time

on our return   many miles from the beach
I would stick my head out the window
I knew I was the one who could
smell it farthest away
I would say: I can smell the sea

there were three long folds of skin
on either side of his mouth
when my Uncle Guicho laughed

4.
in the afternoon
we and the neighbors   would drift
out of our houses to fish
we all would sit on the shore
on large barnacled posts nailed to the edge
with ladders reaching to the water
our fathers or grandfathers   smoking
their cigars to one side of their mouths

the gradual fall of the sun
made us swallow our words
as if we were the ones swallowing the sun
at times one person or another would cry out   feeling
the rod slip in his hand
we children would run to see
to see the half moon that had been caught
always the same   all of them with eyes that never closed
without speaking   we, the children
would draw our feet from the water
as long rectangles of light stretched
from the houses across the gravel road
and to our backs   we knew
that water could swallow you
into nightmares now   it was the place
out of where night rose and was absorbed
into the air   it was the hour
in which one could not have any faith in the sea
or in familiar daytime things

we made the world smaller
and brought it inside in our buckets
with the blue and silver fish
we fried in lard
until the eyes turned white
like the snow we had never seen

5.
the house trembled with my coughs
and the breaths of my phantoms of the night

*Recuerdo . . .

recuerdo un viejo fuerte,
con hombros anchos, alma llena,
y palabras que iluminaban mi vida

y tal hombre era
padre mio,
fuerte y cariñoso
como lamento cantado/llorado
ú consejo amoroso declamado . . .
hombre maduro y macho,
sin temor al mundo él vivía;
padre mío
puro hombre
un chicano orgulloso . . .
en aquellos tiempos . . .
cuando
los militantes presentes
eran aún conservadores.
él ya era protestador . . .

east el paso lo respetaba,
barelas albuquerque lo conoció
en el nacimiento de este siglo,
        él entonces era asote,
        chicano que no se cuarteaba,

era Pedro Lucero Sánchez,
        su madre era Gurulé por apellido,
y él fué
        padre del barrio del diablo (en el paso) ;

era yonquero de los mejores,
        a nadie se le postraba,
su mundo lo admiraba . . .
        ese hombre fue mi padre

34

lo que hoy me puede, carnales,
es tristesa del corazón—
el día que lo entierraron
yo estava hundido en prisión. . . .

—*Ricardo Sánchez*

I REMEMBER

I remember a strong old man,
with wide shoulders, a full soul,
and words that illuminated my life

and such a man was
my father
strong and loving
like a lament sung/cried
or loving advice proclaimed
a man who was mature and masculine,
without fear of the world he lived;
my father
a real man
a proud chicano . . .
in those times . . .
when
present-day militants
were still conservatives.
he was already a protestor . . .

east el paso respected him,
barelas [a barrio in Albuquerque] knew him
in the birth of this century
    at that time he was number one,
    a chicano who never went back on his word,

was Pedro Lucero Sánchez
    his mother's maiden name was Gurulé,
and he was
    the father of el diablo barrio (in el paso);
he was one of the best junk yard dealers,
    nobody ever humiliated him,
his world admired him . . .
    this man was my father

what affects me today, my brothers,
is sadness of heart—
the day they buried him
I was submerged in prison. . . .

*Canto Pa' Mis Amiguitos

(el quinto grado de
Jefferson school, Sanger, Calif.)

mis morenitos curiosos,
you were as quiet as flowers
as you sat and listened to me,
the big man with the beard.

all of you listened to the poem
of my grandmother, went with me
to Payless market, and held hands
as we counted to see

how much our pesetas would buy.
mis niños quietos,
chiquitos, recién llegados
desde el amor de sus padres,

me escucharon como si fuera
famoso o alguien importante.
les leí los poemas
de mi alma con mucho cariño,

y quise llorar cuando
me dijeron que siempre les gustó . . .
hijitos, como me gustó
la clase de ustedes,

como me gustó sentarme
como Santo Clos pa' hablar
con todos ustedes.
deveras, así me sentí,

giving all of you poems as if they were presents . . .
in the playground
i worried and hoped
you wouldn't hurt yourselves

37

as you all swung and climbed . . .
for a moment there in the windy,
cloudy day, i wanted to hug
all of you, keep you all warm

in my coat, give you hot chocolate con canela
and tortillas with butter, hold you
like i hold my little girl,
whisper to all of you

que todos eran mis hijos,
mis huercos mocosos
con cachetes rosados por
el aire, mis niños que siempre

sonríen cuando les leo los poemas
de nuestras familias . . .
ya ustedes me conocen,
ya saben lo que pienso

y lo que siento, lo que me gusta de
comer: pan dulce, burritos como
los hacen nuestras madres,
calientitos y llenos de chile y queso—

tambien el menudo, el cocido con elote
y todas nuestras favoritas comidas . . .
y al fin, ya saben como me miro,
un gordito con barbas que le

gusta sentarse pa' hablar con niños;
un hombre gordo que ustedes sorprendieron
con el amor inocente, un amor que espero
que existe en mis pardos poemas,

amor de los niños del quinto grado,
un amor del que nunca me olvido,
un amor que solamento viene
de los corazones puros de los niños

de la clase de Señora Márquez . . .
pa' todos ustedes, pa' sus familias
que trabajan tan duro,
pa' sus padres

que les han enseñado
tanto sentimiento, les doy
este pobre poema que no empieza a darles
lo que siento yo de ustedes, mis amiguitos . . .

—*Leonard Adame*

SONG FOR MY LITTLE FRIENDS

(the fifth grade of
Jefferson school, Sanger, Calif.)

my inquisitive little brown children,
you were as quiet as flowers
as you sat and listened to me,
the big man with the beard.

all of you listened to the poem
of my grandmother, went with me
to Payless market, and held hands
as we counted to see

how much our money would buy.
my quiet children,
little ones, recently arrived
from your parents' love,

39

you listened to me as if i were
famous or someone important.
i read you the poems
of my soul with much affection,

and i wanted to cry when
you told me that you liked them anyway . . .
little children, how i liked
your class,

how i liked sitting
like Santa Claus to talk
with all of you.
truly, that's how i felt,

giving all of you poems as if they were presents . . .
in the playground
i worried and hoped
you wouldn't hurt yourselves

as you all swung and climbed . . .
for a moment there in the windy,
cloudy day, i wanted to hug
all of you, keep you all warm

in my coat, give you hot chocolate with cinnamon
and tortillas with butter, hold you
like i hold my little girl,
whisper to all of you

that you were all my children,
my little runny-nosed brats
with cheeks rosy from
the fresh air, my children who always

smiled when i read you poems
about our families . . .
you still know me,
you still know what i think

and what i feel, what i like
to eat: sweet cakes, burritos like
our mothers make,
warm and filled with chile and cheese—

also menudo, stew with fresh corn
and all our favorite dishes . . .
and finally, you still know what i look like,
a fat little man with a beard who

likes to sit and talk with children;
a big man whom you surprised
with innocent love, a love that i hope
exists in my brown poems,

love for the children in the fifth grade,
a love i won't ever forget,
a love that comes only
from the pure hearts of the children

of Señora Márquez' class . . .
for all of you, for your families
who work so hard,
for your parents

who have taught you
so much feeling, i give you
this poor poem that doesn't begin to give you
what i feel about you, my little friends . . .

The Old Man Who Is Gone Now

The old man—
He is gone now,
drinking the waters
of death with
the new dead.

Pluto has the
new dead all collected,
in rows and stacks and stacks,
feeding them from the
communal umbilical cord,
Saving one place of honor for
The old man—
He is gone now.

His teeth were gone,
and his gums would bleed
like soft tornados.
Now flowing fast
and then
flash! no pain   no ooze
    Nothing!

The likker that he fancied
smoothed his wounded male pride
and calmed his thoughts
    enough
so that he didn't notice,
or wasn't bothered
by the barbed wire
or the b i a or
    Nothing!

One day he chewed three buttons
and flew backwards and away,
to visit with his Grandpa—
Took the better part of one whole day.

His abuelo said,
"Welcome, mighty warrior.
Come and let us hunt
and feast
and make new babies
to carry on our race."

And so the young warrior
who was an old man
began his peaceful journey
to the waterhole of the dead,
whining softly like
the spirit of the evening breeze.

The Old Man
fancied a dream was life:
The living are really dead
and only pretend to live,
    Or
Do we come alive
only after life has left us?

The Old Man,
He is gone now,
drinking the waters
of death with
the new dead.

—*Margarita Baldenegro Reyes*

---

b i a: Bureau of Indian Affairs
abuelo: grandfather

THE STREETS
OF THE BARRIO

THE STREETS OF THE BARRIO

"Here in the barrios we can open up, be ourselves, and be funny in a Chicano sort of way. We can use both Spanish and English to twist around the obvious. And we can be sad and cry in a way that does not make us feel weak.

"In the barrios I can walk down these streets and know that always somebody will call out my name. The postman is a family friend, and the owner of the corner store will give me credit because he knows I am not going to skip town. Summer nights are the times when all the neighborhood doors are open and the barrio is especially alive. People are on their porches, music blares from open windows and circles of brown children slurp snow cones and play games. So much is happening, so many people are friendly, there is so much to experience and learn.

"True there is death and violence here but there is much more life. . . . Drugs and gang warfare are a part of life in the barrios, but they are not at its heart."

LUIS RODRIGUEZ, "Over There in East L.A.,"
L.A. Weekly

In The Plaza We Walk

In the plaza we walk
under the Mexican moon
full of tangerine smells.

A cart pulls over
full of the fruit
full of the moon
      and the lonely star.

So we buy two
but he says "three for a peso"
      but we buy two.

Tangerines peeled
      we walk
    hand in hand
    spitting the seeds
      for future tangerines
  and more lovers to be.

In the plaza we walk
    under tangerine moons.

—Nephtalí De León

*Lowriders #2

lowriders
cruising the barrio
se vale

sávila pa las quemadas
carmen
for everything else

eating nopales
for breakfast

a besándote
when you
smell like cilantro

todo se vale
todo
hace
su sonido

—*Reyes Cárdenas*

LOWRIDERS #2

lowriders
cruising the barrio
have their value

aloe vera for burns
carmen
for everything else

eating cactus
for breakfast

to kissing you
when you
smell like cilantro

everything has its value
everything
makes
its music

---

cilantro: fresh coriander, used in cooking

*La Peluqueria Del Maestro

Al lado de la iglesia Apostólica de Dios,
cruzando la calle de la iglesia Católica,
se encontraba la peluquería del maestro
donde iba el jefe a cortarse la greña.
Todos los conocidos llegaban sobre la mañana
saludándose uno al otro como amigos que eran
the barrio aristocracy, los hombres de
juicio y de sueños, Lucky Lager instead
of Mint Juleps.
El Maestro con su misma cara todos los sábados;
fuerte, redonda, chimuelo, but kept smiling,
el gran oído, con noble manos
valiendo oro enredadas entre el pelo.
Los sueños de mejoramiento eran realidad
en la peluquería del maestro.
Allí sobre el espejo, un retrato del
muchacho García que pichó por los
Cleveland Indians era la confirmación.

—*Ricardo Vásquez*

THE MAESTRO'S BARBER SHOP

Next to the Apostolic Church of God,
crossing the street where the Catholic church was located,
was the barber shop of the maestro
where my father went to have his hair cut.
All the old acquaintances arrived during the morning
greeting one another like the friends they were
the barrio aristocracy, men of
wisdom and of dreams, Lucky Lager instead
of Mint Juleps.
The Maestro with the same face every Saturday;
strong, round, some teeth missing, but kept smiling,
the great listener, with noble hands
worth gold entangled in their hair.
Dreams of better things to come were a reality
in the maestro's barber shop.
There over the mirror, a photograph of the
García boy who pitched for the
Cleveland Indians was the confirmation.

---

maestro has no English equivalent; the word means skilled workman, master
craftsman

*Nuestro Barrio

nuestro barrio
    en las tardes de paredes grabadas
    los amores de pedro con virginia
    en las tardes
        barriendo
dust about
    swept away in the wind of our breath
el suspiro de dios por nuestras calles
    gravel side streets of solitude
    the mobs from the tracks are coming
en la tarde
    mientras don jose barre su acera
    mientras dios respira vientos secos
        en el barrio sopla la vejez de chon
    y la juventud de juan madura
en la tarde de polvo
    el recuerdo de mi abuelo
    —de las flores en su tumba
    dust
        polvosas flores
blowing free to powdered cruces

—Alurista

OUR BARRIO

our barrio
    in the afternoons of written-on walls
    the loves of Pedro for Virginia
    in the afternoons
        sweeping
dust about
    swept away in the wind of our breath
the sighing of god through our streets
    gravel side streets of solitude
    the mobs from the tracks are coming
in the afternoon
    while don josé sweeps his sidewalk
    while god breathes dry winds
        in the barrio sighs the old age of chon
    and the youth of juan grown up
in the afternoon of dust
    the memory of my grandfather
    —of the flowers on his tomb
    dust
        dusty flowers
blowing free to powdered crosses

*En El Barrio

en el barrio
—en las tardes de fuego
when the dusk prowls
    en la calle desierta
pues los jefes y jefas
    trabajan
        —often late hours
after school
    we play canicas
in the playground
    abandoned and dark
sin luces
    hasta la noche
we play canicas
    until we grow
to make borlote
and walk the streets
con luces
paved—with buildings
altos como el fuego
    —el que corre en mis venas

—Alurista

In The Barrio

in the barrio
—on fiery afternoons*
when the dusk prowls
    in the deserted street
well the mothers and fathers
    work
       —often late hours
after school
    we play marbles
in the playground
    abandoned and dark
without lights
    until night
we play marbles
    until we grow
to make our own party; a wild time
and walk the streets
with lights
paved—with buildings
as tall as the fire
    —the one that courses through my veins

---

fuego can also mean passion

¡Ese!
Within your will-to-be culture,
incisive,
aguzado,
clutching the accurate click &
fist-warm slash of your *filero*
   (hardened equalizer gave you life,
opened up counter-cultures U.S.A.) .

Precursor.

Vato loco alivianado—a legend in your
own time flaunting early Mod, sleazy,
but rigid,
with a message,
in a movement of your own,
in your gait sauntering,
            swaying,
            leaning the wrong way
            in assertion.

Baroque carriage between
waving-to-the-wind ducktails &
double-sole *calcos*
buttressing street-corners as any would-be
pillar of society.
Ethics existential:
            la lisa unbuttoned,
            zoot-suit with pegged *tramos,*
            a thin belt holding up the
            scars of your age—
a moving target for *la jura* brutality;
brown anathema of high-school principals.

Your fierce stance

    vs.

       starched voices:

       "Take those taps off!"
       "Speak English damn it!"
       "Button up your shirt!"
       "When did you last cut your hair?"
       "Coach, give this punk 25 licks!"

Emotion surging silent on your stoic tongue;
machismo-ego punished, feeling your fearful
eyes turn blue in their distant stare.

Day to day into the night, back to back grief,
& the railroad tracks a / Meskin / Dixon line /
hyphenating
the skin of your accent.
Sirol, you heard the train on time
                tearing
through every map of hope SW U.S.A.,
but your poised blood, aware, in a
bitter coming-of-age: a juvenile *la causa*
in your wicked
       stride . . .

      —*Tino Villanueva*

¡Ese!: Man!
aguzado: alert, hip
filero: knife
Vato loco alivianado: exceptional number one guy
calcos: heavy shoes
la lisa: the shirt
tramos: pants
la jura: the police
machismo: male
Sirol: yes
la causa: revolutionary cause

*El Louie

Hoy enterraron al Louie

And San Pedro o sanpinche
are in for it. And those
times of the forties
and the early fifties
lost un vato de atolle.

Kind of slim and drawn,
there toward the end,
aging fast from too much
booze y la vida dura. But
class to the end.

En Sanjo you'd see him
sporting a dark topcoat
playing in his fantasy
the role of Bogart, Cagney
or Raft.

Era de Fowler el vato,
carnal del Candi y el
Ponchi—Los Rodriguez—
The Westside knew 'em
and Selma, even Gilroy.

48 Fleetline, two-tone—
buenas garras and always
rucas—como la Mary y
la Helen . . . siempre con
liras bien afinadas
cantando La Paloma, la
que andaba en el florero.

Louie hit on the idea in
those days for tailor-made

drapes, unique idea—porque
Fowler no era nada como
Los, o'l E.P.T. Fresno's
westside was as close as
we ever got to the big time,

But we had Louie and the
Palomar, el boogie, los
mambos y cuatro suspiros
del alma—y nunca faltaba
the gut-shrinking love-
splitting, ass-hole-up
tight-bad news—

    Trucha, esos! Va 'ber
    pedo!
    Abusau, ese!
    Get Louie
No llores, Carmen, we can
handle 'em.
    Ese, 'on tal Jimmy?
    Horale, Louie
    Where's Primo?
    Va 'ber catos!

En el parking lot away from
the jura.

    Horale!
    Trais filero?
    Simon!
    Nel!
    Chale, ese!
    Oooooh, este vato!

And Louie would come through—
melodramatic music, like in the
mono—tan tan taran!—Cruz

Diablo, El Charro Negro! Bogart
smile (his smile as deadly as
his vaisas!) He dug roles, man,
and names—like blackie, little
Louie . . .

Ese Louie . . .
Chale, call me "Diamonds," man!
Y en Korea fue soldado de
levita con huevos and all the
paradoxes del soldado raso—
heroism and the stockade!

And on leave, jump boots
shainadas and ribbons, cocky
from the war, strutting to
early mass on Sunday morning.

Wow, is that el Louie

Mire, comadre, ahi va el hijo
de Lola!

Afterward he and fat Richard
would hock their bronze stars
for pisto en el Jardin Canales
y en el Trocadero.

At barber college he came
out with honors. Despues
empenaba su velardo de la
peluca pa' jugar pocar serrada
and lo ball en Sanjo y Alviso.

And "Legs Louie Diamond" hit
on some lean times . . .

Hoy enterraron al Louie.

Y en Fowler at Nesei's
pool parlor los baby chooks
se acuerdan de Louie, el carnal
del Candi y el Ponchi—la vez
que lo fileriaron en el Casa
Dome y cuando se catio con La Chiva.

Hoy enterraron al Louie.

His death was an insult
porque no murio en accion—
no lo mataron los vatos,
ni los gooks en Korea.
He died alone in a rented
room—perhaps like a
Bogart movie.

The end was a cruel hoax.
But his life had been
remarkable!

Vato de atolle, el Louie Rodriguez.

—*José Montoya*

LOUIE

Louie was buried today

And San Pedro or sanwhatever
are in for it. And those
times of the forties
and the early fifties
lost a number one guy.

Kind of slim and drawn,
there toward the end,
aging fast from too much
booze and the hard life. But
class to the end.

In San Jose you'd see him
sporting a dark topcoat
playing in his fantasy
the role of Bogart, Cagney
or Raft.

He was from Fowler that guy,
blood-brother of Candi and
Ponchi—the Rodriguez brothers—
The Westside knew 'em
and Selma, even Gilroy.

48 Fleetline, two-tone—
good-looking clothes and always
women—like Mary and
Helen . . . always with
his guitar tuned up
singing La Paloma, and about the girl
who walked in the flower garden.

Louie hit on the idea in
those days for tailor-made

drapes, unique idea—because
Fowler was nothing like
Los Angeles, or El Paso, Texas. Fresno's
westside was as close as
we ever got to the big time,

But we had Louie and the
Palomar, boogie,
mambos and four sighs
of the soul—and there was never any lack of
the gut-shrinking love-
splitting, ass-hole-up
tight-bad news—

    Watch out, guys! There's going
    to be shit!
    Be sharp, man!
    Get Louie
Don't cry, Carmen, we can
handle 'em.
    Man, where's Jimmy?
    Hey, Louie
    Where's Primo?
    There's going to be a fight!

In the parking lot away from
the police.

    Hey!
    Did you bring a knife?
    Yes!
    No!
    Forget it, man!
    Oooooh, that guy!

And Louie would come through—
melodramatic music, like in the
movie theater—tan tan taran!—the Devil
Cross, the Black Rider! Bogart

smile (his smile as deadly as
his fists!) He dug roles, man,
and names—like blackie, little
Louie . . .

Hey Louie . . .
No, call me "Diamonds," man!
And in Korea he was a soldier in
uniform with balls and all the
paradoxes of the ordinary G.I.—
heroism and the stockade!

And on leave, jump boots
shined and ribbons, cocky
from the war, strutting to
early mass on Sunday morning.

Wow, is that Louie

Look, comadre, there goes
Lola's son!

Afterward he and fat Richard
would hock their bronze stars
for liquor in the Jardin Canales
and in the Trocadero.

At barber college he came
out with honors. Afterwards
he pawned his wig stand
to play poker
and lo ball in San Jose and Alviso.

And "Legs Louie Diamond" hit
on some lean times . . .

Today Louie was buried.

And in Fowler at Nesei's
pool parlor the baby pachucos
are remembering Louie, blood-brother
of Candi and Ponchi—the time
they knifed him at the Casa
Dome and when he fought with La Chiva.

Today Louie was buried.

His death was an insult
because he didn't die in action—
he wasn't killed by other gang members
nor by gooks in Korea.
He died alone in a rented
room—perhaps like a
Bogart movie.

The end was a cruel hoax.
But his life had been
remarkable!

A number one guy, Louie Rodriguez.

---

comadre: expression of friendship or kinship

AQUELLOS VATOS

Simón,
we knew him as la Zorra—uncouth but
squared away;
messed around unpaved streets. No different
from el Caballo de Littlefield, or from
la Chiva de McAllen who never let himself down;
always had a movida chueca somewhere up town.
Then there was la Polla de San Anto— lived
across the creek, y tenía un ranfle sentao
pa' tras, ¿me entiendes?
And el Pato de Nuquis, el que se la madereaba;
and la Rata was already growing a mouse-tache at
early ten.
El Conejo estaba todo locote, y era más largo
que no sé qué; had rucas all over the place, man:
not even Don Juan carried a rabbit's foot.
El Bear se salía del cuadro; he was forever
polishing his Cat's Paw double-sole derechonas,
and heterosexual la Perra used to snicker and
warn in Spanish—"You keep bending down like *that*
Bear, and you'll wind up in dallas."

Chale,
I don't recall el Tiger . . . they tell me he was
a chavalón que se curaba con las gabas.
I do remember el Gorrión, un carnal a todo dar—
never said much, but his tattoos were sure a
conversation piece.
¿A la Burra? ¡qué gacho le filorearon la madre
en el chancleo! and el Canario went to the pinta
for it. Not to Sing Sing but the State Farm is
just as bad. La palomilla hasn't been the same since.

They've probably married by now,
those cats,
and their kids try to comprehend culture and

identity by reading "See Spot. See Spot run,"
and by going to the zoo on a Greyhound bus with
Miss Foxx.

—*Tino Villanueva*

(Note: all of the vatos—members of this particular *palomilla* or group of friends—have animal nicknames which contribute to the appropriateness of the final stanza:

la Zorra:　the fox
el Caballo:　the horse
la Polla:　the chicken
el Pato:　the duck
la Rata:　the rat
el Conejo:　the rabbit
la Perra:　the dog
el Gorrión:　the sparrow
la Burra:　the donkey)

Simón:　yes
la Chiva:　another member of the group; slang term for heroin
movida chueca:　an illegal deal or activity
y tenía un rafle sentao/pa' tras, ¿me entiendes?:　and had an old car lowered in the rear, know what I mean?
el que se la madereaba:　the one who used to bullshit a lot, who tried to get favors through flattery
estaba todo locote, y era más largo que no sé qué:　was completely crazy, and was bigger than I don't know what
rucas:　women
se salía del cuadro:　left the neighborhood
derechonas:　heavy shoes
chale:　no
a chavalón que se curaba con las gabas:　a guy who used to satisfy himself with Anglo women
un carnal a todo dar:　the greatest person
qué gaucho le filorearon la madre/en el chancleo:　a really bad thing that he knifed at the dance
the pinta:　penitentiary

67

en la tarde del trece
de noviembre por la calle
del barrio México pasó

Joe en su Ford van
bien loco a
     f
      t
       e
        r shooting up some smack
         man, parecía como si
         estaba en la nube número
         99999999999999999999999

                 afuera del parking lot
                 he put his pistola
                 between his belt and pants
                 nobody could tell it
                 was there—ni él mismo!

Adentro del *CIELITO POOL HALL*
estaba toda la palomía:
         el guajolote
         el afro
         el kris
         la rosie
         el matón
         la estrellita
              /
                /
              /entró Joe
               y nomás oía
               el zzzumbido
               //*/*/*/
               en su cabeza

```
*******************************************ta-tum******
****ta-tum**********ta-tum********ta-tum**********
```
oh, give me the beat, boys, and free my soulllllllll
I want to get lost in your rock 'n rolllllllllllllll
and drift awaaaaaaaaaaaaaaaaaaaaaaaaaaaaaaaaaaaaay!

"Joey, ¿traes un toke?"

"Hórale carnal, cómo 'stas?"

"Estoy viajando, ese."

El guajolote, la estrellita,
y el afro se 'rrancaron pa' tras
a sonarse unos tokes.

Joe se sentó adentro
del pool hall en la
silla en una esquina
viendo todo como un
mono bien loco
. . . .

parecía que le estaban
jugando el billar entre
las piernas de la rosie

. . . .

se puso a reir.

"está estrampado el vato otra vez," dijo el kris.

.

_____

I don't dig any puto laughing
when I'm hustling the ball, ese!
(dijo otro bato: el larry: que acababa
de llegar del 'Nam.)

"La fría, Larry. Ese Joe está loco."

.

_____

Oh, so ese es el Joe.
Se cree bien chingón/
el mister big stuff

69

Pues, nadien se va reir
de mí. . . . no damn gook or
anyone else . . . .
                    La rosie le agarró
                    la mano para detenerlo
                    y al mismo tiempo
                    a c a r i c i a r l o.

                                    .
"¡No andes jodiendo!"——————————

"Mira, joven
salte afuera
si quieres pleito

        o   le habló a la jura."

                            Dijo el viejito
                            que se encargaba
                            del CIELITO.

Joe se comenzó a reir
otra vez parecía el
larry como el mono
mickey mouse (apenas en un rollo de colores)

                    Joe miró pa' rriba cuando sintió
                    alguien estirándole las garras.
                    Vió la cara del mickey mouse
                    espumando del hocico

y Joe se rió otra vez.

                            .
                ——————— I just got back from 'Nam
                        Bronze Star and two hearts
                        and no junkie bato is going
                        to laugh in my face, see?
                        I killed two cong with this
                        filero, see?

El lugar estaba bien silencioso
hasta la música se había parado
entraron los otros vatos de afuera
bien sonados y platicando . . . .

  ((hey, ¿quéestá pasando?))

(((el larry anda como loco y le está cantando al Joe)))

                    Adentro se veía el mismo retrato:
                    el larry con la navaja en la mano
                    urgiendo que se moviera Joe en
                    cualquier dirección . . . .

. . . . . . y Joe, todavía
con la sonrisa loca.

                    //man, I don't give a hot damn
                       what you've done ni me importa
                       quien chingón crees que eres.
                       —but you don't treat Rosie like
                       that—you understand?//

El sudor le caía a la cara
y su mano comenzó a temblar
pero lo dijo

                        .
    ——————————— she's a lousy lay
                       you hear that, junkie?
                       l-o-u-s-y, stinking
                                    l o u s y

                    Con éso le brincó a Joe
                    cortándole la piel del brazo
                    la luz arriba de la mesa de
                    billar llevando casi todo
                    el golpe

Hahahahahahahahahahahahahaha

71

                              ...... casi como en s-l-o-w
                                    m-o-t-i-o-n sacó la pistola.

El viejito ni podía
resollar como si le
habían cerrado la garganta
—los otros: helados.

                              Solamente la luz se movía
                              un momento aluzándole la cara
                              al larry y al otro oscureciéndolo.

                                                              .
"damn gook junkie, yahoooooooooooow!" ————————

                              Le brincó a Joe otra vez
                              como un left-end tackle
                              contra los dallas cowboys
                              empujándolo contra la pared
                              puñaleándolo en la pierna
              O   y entonces se oyó el tiro
            OOO
        POOOOOOOW.   Los demás pegaron el piso
            OOO   ni asomándose.
              O

Alguien comenzó a llorar.

                              El larry corrió a la puerta.

Estaba oscuro afuera
menos las luces del
              C*I*N*E A*L*A*M*E*D*A

                              Brillaba el anuncio:

/Gran Estreno/
   HOY

Jalisco No Se Raja
  y
El Principio (a colores)

y Larry herido comenzó
a correr al cine como
una palomía a la llama

Joe se detuvo de la puerta
—sentía el dolor muy lejos
solamente le ardían los
ojos con la luz fuerte del
cine

y vió al larry corriendo
como un pato en la galería
de carabina en el carnaval.

            O
          OOO
PODOOOOOW.
          OOO
            O

                    No voltió para atrás . . . .

//y hay tienen el mono en el canto//

Se puso a reir agarrando
el pañuelo que usaba como
bandana y lo amarró
alrededor de su pierna

Todavía no sentía
el dolor y casi estaba
sangrando . . . .

¿Y ahora para dónde?

Comenzó el van
la música del cartucho
tocando a todo vuelo

******ta-tum****************
*************oh, come on and
take, oh take me************
*****and drift awaaaaaaaaaay.

Primero al canto a
levantar su stash

¿Y de ahí? Puso el turn
signal y tomó el camino del
norte donde quizá no sabían
del mono loco. El polvo del
camino ni se veía en el oscuro.

—*Gregorio Barrios*

CRAZY MOVIE

in the afternoon on the thirteenth
of November along the street
of the Mexican barrio went

Joe in his Ford van
really crazy a
            f
             t
              e
               r shooting up some smack
                man, it seemed like he
                was on cloud number
                99999999999999999999

outside in the parking lot
he put his pistol
between his belt and pants
nobody could tell it
was there—not even himself!

74

Inside the *CIELITO POOL HALL*
was the whole gang:

                    turkey
                    afro
                    kris
                    rosie
                    killer
                    estrellita
                              /
                               /
                                /Joe went in
                                hearing only
                                the buzzzzzz
                                //*/*/*/
                                in his head

ta-tum****
****ta-tum**********ta-tum********ta-tum***********
oh, give me the beat, boys, and free my soulllllllll
I want to get lost in your rock 'n rolllllllllllllll
and drift awaaaaaaaaaaaaaaaaaaaaaaaaaaaaaaaaaaaaaaaaay!

"Joey, did you bring a toke?"

                              "Hey brother, how are you?"

"I'm tripping, man."

                    turkey, estrellita,
                    and afro went off out in back
                    to blow some tokes.

Joe sat inside
the pool hall in a
chair in the corner
watching everything like a
really crazy movie . . . .
                    it seemed to him like they were
                    playing billiards between
                    rosie's legs . . . .
                              he began to laugh.
                    75

"the guy's wasted again," said kris.

.

——————

        I don't dig any faggot laughing
        when I'm hustling the ball, man!
        (said the other dude: larry: who had just
        gotten back from 'Nam.)

"Cool it, Larry. That guy Joe is crazy."

      .
—————————— Oh, so that guy is Joe.
        He thinks he's really top dude/
        mister big stuff
        well, nobody's going to laugh
        at me. . . . no damn gook or
        anyone else. . . . .
                rosie held tight to
                his hand to stop him
                and at the same time
                to caress him.

                .
"Don't let it bother you!"——————————

"Look, kid
go outside
if you want to fight

        or I'll call the cops."

           Said the old guy
           who ran
           the CIELITO.

Joe started to laugh
once again larry looked to him
like a mickey mouse film
(barely in color)

76

Joe looked up when he felt
someone pulling at his clothes.
He saw mickey mouse's face
foaming at the mouth

and Joe laughed again.

————— I just got back from 'Nam
Bronze Star and two hearts
and no junkie dude is going
to laugh in my face, see?
I killed two cong with this
knife, see?

The place was very silent
even the music had stopped
the others came in from outside
very stoned and talking. . . . . . .

((hey, what's happening?))

(((larry is acting crazy and he's picking a fight with Joe)))

Inside is the same scene:
larry with the knife in his hand
daring Joe to make a move of
any kind. . . . .

. . . . . .and Joe,
with the same crazy smile.

//man, I don't give a hot damn
what you've done it doesn't matter to me
how important you think you are.
—but you don't treat Rosie like
that—you understand?//

The sweat was running down his face
and his hand began to shake
but he said it

———————————— she's a lousy lay
you hear that, junkie?
l-o-u-s-y, stinking
                    l o u s y

With that he leaped at Joe
cutting the skin on his arm
the light over the
billiard table taking almost all of
the blow

Hahahahahahahahahahahahaha

      . . . . . . almost as if in s-l-o-w
                 m-o-t-i-o-n he drew out the pistol.

The old man could scarcely
breathe as if someone had
closed off his throat
—the others: frozen.

            Only the light was moving
            one moment illuminating larry's face
            and the other leaving it in darkness.

"damn gook junkie, yahoooooooooooow!" ————————————

            He leaped at Joe again
            like a left-end tackle
            against the dallas cowboys
            pushing him against the wall
            stabbing him in the leg
      O   and then a shot was heard
     OOO
POOOOOOOW.
     OOO
      O   The others hit the floor
            not looking up.

78

Someone began to cry.

                    Larry ran to the door.

It was dark outside
except for the lights of the
                    A*L*A*M*E*D*A T*H*E*A*T*E*R

                    The sign shone:

/ Grand Premiere/
    TODAY

Jalisco Doesn't Back Down
                    and
The Beginning (in color)

                              and Larry wounded began
                              to run toward the movie theater like
                              a moth toward the flame

Joe propped himself against the door
—very far away he felt the pain
only his eyes burned
from the strong light of the
movie theater

                              and he saw larry running
         O   like a duck in a
       OOO   carnival shooting gallery.
POOOOOOOW.
       OOO
         O   He didn't turn back. . . . .

//and there you have the movie in the song//

                              He burst out laughing grabbing
                              the handkerchief that he used as
                              a bandana and tied it
                              around his leg

He still didn't feel
the pain and he was hardly
bleeding. . . . .

                    And now where?

The van began playing
the music on the cartridge
at full volume

                    ******ta-tum*****************
                    *************oh, come on and
                    take, oh take me************
                    *****and drift awaaaaaaaaaay.

First home to
get his stash

                    And from there? He pushed the turn
signal and took the road heading
north where maybe nobody knew
about the crazy movie. The dust from
the road was invisible in the dark.

EL MUNDO

EL MUNDO

"There is a heat more intense than the fire of the torch!" Clemente cried cheerfully. "And it can be rekindled at a moment's notice! Wherever discrimination and injustice and oppression rear their ugly heads the fire can be called upon to burn them away! Wherever there is an honest man, a poor man, an oppressed man, the fire smoulders in his heart, ready to ignite and light his path! It is the fire of love that burns in each man and woman and child; it is the fire of the soul of our people which must serve us now!"

RUDOLFO A ANAYA, Heart of Aztlán

*Must Be The Season Of The Witch

must be the season of the witch
        la bruja
        la llorona
she lost her children
        and she cries
en las barrancas of industry
        her children
devoured by computers
and the gears
must be the season of the witch
        i hear huesos crack
in pain
        y lloros
la bruja pangs
        sus hijos han olvidado
la magia de durango
        y la de moctezuma
        —el huiclamina
must be the season of the witch
la bruja llora
sus hijos sufren: sin ella

—*Alurista*

83

MUST BE THE SEASON OF THE WITCH

must be the season of the witch
            the witch
            la llorona*
she lost her children
            and she cries
in the canyons of industry
            her children
devoured by computers
and the gears
must be the season of the witch
            i hear bones crack
in pain
            and sobbing
the witch pangs
            her children have forgotten
the magic of durango
            and that of moctezuma
            —the huiclamina
must be the season of the witch
the witch cries
her children suffer: without her

La llorona is a Medea-like figure in Mexican folklore; having lost, drowned, or killed her children—several versions of the legend exist—she can be heard at night weeping and mourning for their return.

DOPEFIENDS TRIP

What you call me, man?
"A vicious, dangerous criminal!"
Huh?

Man, you are wrong
I ain't nothing
        but
                a pest to society
An insignificant dud
Who got caught
In this here shit called crime

A stone junkie
     Whose high
Ends up congesting the States prisons
I do my little time on the streets
Petty thievery
     Loaded out my mind
Then back to the pen
To do my life
On the installment plan
Payments paid daily in;
A.M.'s and P.M.'s

Pass the salt, brother
    It might help
        This here prison stew......

                  —Hector Angulo

$

one dollar down
and one por los siglos de los siglos
way of life
of the so much per hour
and five dollars a baptism generation,
prices going up to heaven
instead of prayers.
insufficient funds,
gasoline and meat
                No no más no como yo
                sino que ni mi carro bebe.
dollar devaluation
god and gold and silver
                at an all time high
more taxes, less work
              tighter control
phase III of face I and II that didn't work
phase IV lurks
trigo to russia
            lumber to japan
                  b-52's to cambodia
(i wonder if they fly on the same gas i don't have)
shower every other day
and water your lawn with beer
don't iron and watch tv at the same time,
cook on the sidewalk with el calor de sol,
sulphur and lead added freely to the free air,
the general electric demon joining el paso natural gas
which in turn joins humble oil
and all the demons of the dollar sign
preparing for a final feast
                with all of us

(ya ni podemos decir . . . dale gas . . .)
  no no más te sales, carnal . . . te vas.

—Abelardo

---

por los siglos de los siglos: for centuries to come
no no más no come yo/sino que ni mi carro bebe: no, I don't eat any more
    but my car doesn't drink any more either
trigo: wheat
el calor del sol: the sun's heat
ya ni podemos decir . . .:   now we can't even say
dale gas: let's get going (lit. "give it the gas")
no no más te sales, carnal . . . te vas: no, you don't just get out, brother . . .
    you go away forever.

From 22 I see my first 8 weren't.
   Around the 9th, I was called "meskin."
      By the 10th, I knew and believed I was.
         I found out what it meant to know, to believe . . .
                       before my 13th.
Through brown eyes, seeing only brown colors and feeling
only brown feelings . . . I saw . . . I felt . . . I hated
. . . I cried . . . I tried . . . I didn't understand during
                       these 4.
     I rested by just giving up.
While, on the side . . . I realized I BELIEVED in
   white as pretty,
     my being governor,
       blond blue eyed baby Jesus,
         cokes and hamburgers,
            equality for all regardless of race, creed, or color,
           Mr. Williams, our banker.
        I had to!
      That was all I had.
Beans and Communism were bad.
         Past the weeds, atop the hill, I looked back.
Pretty people, combed and squeaky clean, on
                    arrowlike roads.
Pregnant girls, ragged brats, swarthy machos, rosary beads,
and friends waddle clumsily over and across hills,
               each other,
mud, cold, and woods on caliche ruts.
At the 19th mile, I fought blindly at everything and
               anything.
  Not knowing, Not caring about WHY, WHEN, or
              FOR WHAT.
  I fought. And fought.
    By the 21st, I was tired and tried.

But now. . . .
I've been told that I am dangerous.
That is because I am good at not being a Mexican.
That is because I know now that I have been cheated.
That is because I hate circumstances and love choices.

You know . . . chorizo tacos y tortillas ARE good,
                                             even at school.

Speaking Spanish is a talent.
Being Mexican IS as good as Rainbo bread.
And without looking back, I know that there are still
                                             too many . . .

brown babies,
    pregnant girls,
        old 25-year-old women,
            drunks,
                who should have lived but didn't,
                    on those caliche ruts.

        It is tragic that my problems during these past
                                             21 miles
            were/are/might be . . .
                looking into blue eyes,
                wanting to touch a gringita,
                ashamed of being Mexican,
            believing I could not make it at college,
        pretending that I liked my side of town,
        remembering the Alamo,
    speaking Spanish in school bathrooms only,
and knowing that Mexico's prostitutes like Americans
                                             better.
At 22, my problems are still the same but now I know I am
                                             your problem.
That farm boys, Mexicans and Negro boys are in Vietnam is
                        but one thing I think about:
                Crystal City, Texas 78839
                The migrant worker;
                The good gringo:

89

Staying Mexican enough;
Helping;
Looking at the world from the back of a truck.
The stoop labor with high school rings on their fingers;
The Anglo cemetery,
Joe the different Mexican,
                    Damn.
                    Damn.
                    Damn.

                              —*José Angel Gutiérrez*

---

gringita: white girl
caliche: white hard soil, a mixture of lime and dirt
gringo: Anglo-American

*M'IJO NO MIRA NADA

—Mira, m'ijo, qué rascacielo.
   "Does it reach the sky and heaven?"
—Mira, m'ijo, qué carrazo.
   "Can it get to the end of the world?"
—Mira, m'ijo, ese soldado.
   "¿Por qué pelea?"
—Mira, m'ijo, qué bonita fuente.
   "Yes, but I want to go to the restroom."
—Mira, m'ijo, qué tiendota de J.C. Penney,
   allí trabajarás un día.
   "Do you know the people there, daddy?"
—No
   vámonos a casa,
   tú no miras nada.

                              —*Tomás Rivera*

MY SON DOESN'T SEE A THING

—Look, son, what a skyscraper.
   "Does it reach the sky and heaven?"
—Look, son, what a fine car.
   "Can it get to the end of the world?"
—Look, son, see that soldier.
   "Why does he fight?"
—Look, son, what a beautiful fountain.
   "Yes, but I want to go to the restroom."
—Look, son, what an enormous J.C. Penney store,
   there is where you will work one day.
   "Do you know the people there, daddy?"
—No
   let's go home,
   you can't see a thing.

THE SPANISH GIRLS

the spanish girls are not getting
any braver
they ride backwards as they always did
on the subways
with their bright orange faces
and their hair of black shellac
you can still put your hand
inside one of their eyes
and feel the cold metal of the hook
or the worn surface of a stone
that has been bathed on the moon
you can still fit your body
inside their mouths and
sense the origin of death
as if it were nothing more common
than the turning of a light bulb
or the plaster on the wall
you can still dance with them
back to back as they go on
pursuing your sex with
the cunning of an insane nun
you can even ride them like horses
beaten in the snow
and smell their blood welling up
until it crystallizes in your nostrils
you can go ahead and eat them
with your electrolic spoons and knives
as they arch and shudder on your lip
you can still use them
like instruments of war
that glint nationally blue in the dawn
weeping at the distance of their feet
at the immensity of their hands
the spanish girls aren't getting
any braver
just somehow smaller

from having dwelled for so long
inside the poet's nerve
obsessed with the sickness of guitars
and with the wounds of bulls

—Iván Argüelles

THE MAN OF O

Juan who has eaten circles all his life
begins to speak, his mouth a wide oval,
all those tortillas, all those beans.
He sits before this job-man,
the one whose name is John who has ingested
bread, square pictures in dark gold frames.
The man of O chants his children's names:
"Rosa, José, Jaime, Alejandro . . ." and the
stops form a circle, his family, his other bread.
He lists his jobs before lay-offs,
the parabola of uncertainty.
He and his friends have stood together in abrazo
shoulder to shoulder, arms laced, heads close,
their warm, leaning love a rainbow.
All of John's life, bread, bread. What does it do
to him . . . he opens his mouth and out come
paragraphs of four questions. They form the block
a question mark at each corner.
There on his desk the square frame:
the four corners of his life,
wife, son, daughter, self.
In his heart the stations of his cross:
in the name of the third, and of the sixth,
and of the ninth and twelfth hours.
Some say John's bread is green paper,
that he makes it himself and signs his name,
that his bread, store-bought, never changes
as the brown man's maps, spread by hands he kisses,
maps with eyes often burned.
The man of bread meets his friends and one extends
his hand to shake while those who wait pose,
three corners of a rectangle.

The brown man begins a song, he is singing rounds:
his family, an illness, stolen car, son in trouble,
and the man of squares says, "Get to the point!"

The brown man again begins his song of n's and r's,
his words a cloud, rounded and opaque:
"It is possible, perhaps, not sure . . ."
and the man of bread says, "Begin at the beginning."
John likes to count, likes to stop by four
whether there is a line or no, whether the line
of brown and black goes clear out and around
the whole square floor and around again.
"It is possible" John's heart is made of
          manila folders.
"Perhaps" the brown man's heart is round like his hat
and never stops as long as his sons bear sons
and his daughters roll round bread-maps.
"I'm not sure" but I say that could the circle-man
complete even one circle-song, not even John, son of John,
could slash it with,
          "No, next!"

                    —*Marina Rivera*

———

abrazo: embrace

Visions Of Mexico While At A Writing Symposium In Port Townsend, Washington

*"This world understands nothing
but words and you have come into it
with almost none."*
—*Antonio Porchia*

México:

When I'm that far south, the old words
molt off my skin, the feathers of
all my nervousness.
My own words somersault naturally as my name,
joyous among all those meadows: Michoacán,
Vera Cruz, Tenochtitlán, Oaxaca . . .
Pueblos green on the low hills
where men slap handballs below acres of maiz.
I watch and understand.
My frail body has never packed mud
or gathered in the full weight of the harvest.
Alone with the women in the adobe, I watch men,
their taut faces holding in all their youth.
This far south we are governed by the laws
of the next whole meal. We work and watch
seabirds elbow their wings
in migratory ways, those mispronouncing gulls
coming south
to refuge or gameland.

I don't want to pretend I know more
and can speak all the names. I can't.
My sense of this land can only ripple through my veins
like the chant of an epic corrido.
I come from a long line of eloquent illiterates
whose history reveals what words don't say.
Our anger is our way of speaking,
the gesture is an utterance more pure than word:
We are not animals
but our senses are keen and our reflexes,
accurate punctuation.

All the knifings in a single night, low-voiced
scufflings, sirens, gunnings . . .
we hear them
and the poet within us bays.

Washington:

I don't belong this far north.
The uncomfortable birds gawk at me.
They hem and haw from their borders in the sky.
I heard them say: Mexico is a stumbling comedy,
a loose-legged Cantinflas woman
acting with Pancho Villa drunkenness.
Last night at the tavern
this was all confirmed
in a painting of a woman: her glowing
silk skin, a halo
extending from her golden coiffure
while around her dark skinned men with Jap slant eyes
were drooling in a caricature of machismo.
Below it, at the bar, two Chicanas
hung at their beers. They had painted black
birds that dipped beneath their eyelids.
They were still as foam while the men
fiddled with their asses, absently;
the bubbles of their teased hair snapped
open in the forced wind of the beating fan.

there are songs in my head I could sing you
songs that could drone away
all the Mariachi bands you thought you ever heard

97

songs that could tell you what I know
or have learned from my people
but for that   I need words
simple black nymphs between white sheets of paper
obedient words   obligatory words   words I steal
in the dark when no one can hear me

as pain sends seabirds south from the cold
I have come north
to gather my feathers
for quills

—Lorna Dee Cervantes

se fueron
por el camino real
ese largo y triste camino de eucaliptos
en carretas con burros
un montón de frijol y maíz
y llegaron en lowered down chevys
with gafas fileros
speaking about the low life
tomando botellas de tequila
que decían Made in Mexico
hablando tres palabras de inglés
apple pie y coffee
cantando
Vámonos a California
Vámonos a California

se iban
por el alambre
indios de calzón blanco y huarache
y aterrizaban
pochos pachucos perdidos
vatos locos con tatuajes mágicos
de vida y muerte
esperando en las esquinas el big hit
the 5 & 10 of caliente race track
that never came
cantando calladitos por las calles iban
Vámonos a California
Vámonos a California

they came
from New York
New York the big apple
to the big orange
Yorubas Jíbaros Borinquens
regando las calles con bacardí

piel color café oscuro
ojos de verde cocodrilo
y un tun-tun de tambores
de viejas selvas ancestrales
que alguna vez fueron
pero ahora con mil memorias
de viajes mal pagados
Vámonos a California
Vámonos a California
Vámonos a California

—Alejandro Murguía

O California

they went
along the Camino Real
that long and sad road of eucalyptus
in carts with donkeys
an enormous heap of beans and corn
and arrived in lowered down chevys
with sunglasses switchblades
speaking about the low life
drinking bottles of tequila
that said Made in Mexico
speaking three words of English
apple pie and coffee
singing
Let's go to California
Let's go to California

they went
through the barbed wire
Indians in white trousers and sandals
and landed
pochos pachucos lost
crazy guys with magical tattoos
of life and death
waiting on corners for the big hit
the 5 & 10 of Caliente Race Track
that never came
singing quietly they went along the streets
Let's go to California
Let's go to California

they came
from New York
New York the big apple
to the big orange
Yorubas Jíbaros Borinquens
watering the streets with Bacardi
skin the color of dark coffee
eyes of crocodile green
and a tun-tun of drums
of old ancestral jungles
that existed at one time
but now with a thousand memories
of voyages badly paid
Let's go to California
Let's go to California
Let's go to California

---

pochos: Mexican-Americans (derogatory)
pachucos: young Chicanos of the early and middle 1940s; "hoods"
Yorubas: native Indians of Puerto Rico
Jíbaros: Puerto Rican peasant farmers
Borinquens: synonym for Puerto Ricans

SMALL TOWNS

    appear out of nowhere
floating above the heat of asphalt highways
shimmering in yellow fields
worked out   canneried out   railroaded out places
mined out and left out towns
old men drinking from paper bag
in front of crumbling hotel
mud caked façade of spanish arches
now housing levi's stores   or banks
at whose entrance young mexicanos gather
khakis and t'shirted
to throw dice & bullshit
a new generation of locos

    small towns beckon on obscure side roads
somewhere never mentioned
WELCOME TO BRADLEY, POP. 100 ELEV. 247
an undreamed of place
riding a thin coating of gravel
under the foothills of San Benito
Tres Pinos on route 154
as it was in the beginning
dotted white line gathers speed
people and fronts become blurs
30's deco face of every small time theatre
in the U.S.A. flips by
    as if in a movie

                    —Alejandro Murguía

HEADING FOR EUGENE

califas
> baby blue skies
> con patches de
> white clouds
> flat fields running
> into famous mountain range

yo yo

> comiendo tacos de
> frijoles

> california winds
> caressing and teasing
> roadside trees

> partially clad fruit
> trees
> like pregnant women
> full and about
> to burst into color
> presenting to the world
> the fruit of their many wombs

todos los canals
> llenos de agua
> los swimming pools
> de Chicanos
> cuantos de
> nuestros niños
> han morido
> jugando contigo

califas music
    los oldies but goodies

have you ever heard of Turlock?
    sitting on MAIN street
    watching Turlockeans
    go about the business
    of living

y yo waiting for a 7-up
    white americans
    con los backpacks
    heading for the freeway

yo y mi 7-up
    heading for the freeway
    volkswagen buses
    abound
    Where would we be
    without Germany?
    There would be six
    million more people
    in the world
    probably half
    of them
    owning volkswagen buses

Heading for Eugene

—Lorenza Schmidt

---

califas: slang term for California
con patches de: with patches of
yo yo comiendo tacos de frijoles: I I eating bean tacos
todos los canals . . . jugando contigo: all the canals filled with water/Chicano swimming pools/how many of our children have died playing with you

man, i felt like running all night

but los pasos son pesados
and my calcos se reniegan de
hacer tanto polvo por el barrio
 (french toes con spit shine y todo)
y se cansa uno de tanto correr . . .
we're always running, man,
always running
como si hubiera un fuego
on the other side of the world
que tenemos que alcansar
in due time
pero la realidad tells us
that the fuego es aquí,
donde vivimos nosotros
and to run from it
is not right, just not right
no pega el jale ese,
but the urge para correr
is there, man, it's always there
como like a dove seeking refuge
in the open sky,
but it's different with the dove, man,
he don't hurt as we hurt
as we try to seek refuge,
y el pájaro no
deja caer lágrimas
as we do, man,
and the lágrimas hacen
lodo with the dust of
the barrio,
y el lodo no deja correr,
you just can't run in
the mud, man—
se chingan los french toes con spit shine

mientras tratamos de establish traction
en el lodo—
no se puede.

—*Salomón R. Baldenegro, Jr.*

MAN, I FELT LIKE RUNNING ALL NIGHT

man, i felt like running all night

but my steps are heavy
and my shoes rebel against
making so much dust for the barrio
(french toes with spit shine and all)
and a man gets tired of running so much . . .
we're always running, man,
always running
as if there were a fire
on the other side of the world
that we have to catch up with
in due time
but reality tells us
that the fire is here,
where we ourselves live
and to run from it
is not right, just not right
the job isn't worth a damn
but the urge to run
is there, man, it's always there
like a dove seeking refuge
in the open sky,
but it's different with the dove, man,
he don't hurt as we hurt
as we try to seek refuge,
and the bird does not
shed tears
as we do, man,
and the tears make
mud with the dust of
the barrio,
and the mud won't let you run,
you just can't run in
the mud, man—
the french toes with spit shine are ruined
while we try to establish traction
in the mud—
it can't be done.

*Ya Estufas

espumado con atoles de nubes
        el cielo colorado
witnessed a dusk
        of murals
        painted
in the spirit
        of liberación nacional
in the spirit
        of the fallen
brown dry leaves
        of autumn
las cananas en
        la tarde
aparecieron and
        thousands
of bullets
        turned
        to flowers,
kissed la raza's heart
        and many Mexicans
cried "ya estufas
        viva la revolución"

—Alurista

GET STUFFED

foamy with clouds like atole
        the red-colored sky
witnessed a dusk
        of murals
        painted
in the spirit
        of national liberation
in the spirit
        of the fallen
brown dry leaves
        of autumn
the cannons in
        the afternoon
appeared and
        thousands
of bullets
        turned
        to flowers,
kissed the heart of the people
        and many Mexicans
cried "get stuffed
        long live the revolution"

---

atole: a warm sweet drink made with corn meal

AND

.... and @ $1.13 + tx
      i couldn't complain
      that my red beans n' rice
      were alive and kicking
      a mean steaming salsa
            they're only a reflection
            of our condition
            and the spirit of our times
      picante como la gente
      pegado like our souls
            (but everybody knows
            that's the best part)
      they were alive
      and telling me
      in ancient unspoken
      tongues of visions
      unseen cooking up
      images of emotions unknown
            then . . .
            with the aroma of a rumba
            and the taste of conga licks
      la revolución
      came swiftly upon me
      on warm rhythms
      and powerful vibrations
            de colores washing
            every pore of my body
            until all that existed
      was raza
      in a chorus of struggle
      and a baile of liberation
            revolution on my tongue
            lingering hot
            como salsa picante,
            sabroso, picoso
      and the visions were grand

of great halls and
band
eras red
and streaming
from every barrio and campo
        and the yanqui
        nowhere to be seen
        not from sea to shining
        rio bravo
and all greyhound stations
faced east
un sentido
sin pepsi-cola
        even the big apple
        shook loose its gusanos
        and waves of spanish smiles
        flooded the air
        and cleansed the soul. . . .
and i say unto you
by static stars
and unmoving heavens
that all this is true
        and verily then
        for the sake of your people
        and the salvation of our kind
        go forth and organize. . . .!
        (but remember to pay the bill) .

—*Ricardo Gonsalves*

---

picante como la gente: feisty like the people
pegado: beaten
baile: dance
como salsa picante,/ sabroso, picoso: like highly seasoned sauce,/ savory,
        strong and sharp
campo: field
un sentido / sin pepsi-cola: a feeling without pepsi-cola
gusanos: worms

*Sobre La Liberacion De La Mujer

And la Mujer sat on
    the curve
And cried: "I am only a woman!"
      "I am defenseless and can do nothing!!"
      "Desgracia la mía ser mujer!"
Y se ahogó en sus propias
    lágrimas y self-pity.

Y encontraron su cuerpo
    cuando se secó el lago de lágrimas
Y dijeron ellos "La pobre se ahogó . . .
    ni modo. . . . . . ."
Y siguieron caminando nodding their heads.

And La Mujer sat on
    the curve.
Y dice: "Pinche concrete curve, cala mucho!!"
    Se levantó y caminó,
    . . . se trompieza con una piedra . . .
Y dice: "Pinche piedra, me machucó el dedo!!"
    Echando madres siguió and
    she bumped into a lampost. . . .
Y dice: "Pinche lampost . . . que harto dolor me dejó!!!"

    PERO. . . . .
Ella siguió y siguió. . . . . . .
Llegó a la casa. . . . . . .
Y se puso a hacer tortillas y Revolución.

        —*María Saucedo*

ABOUT WOMEN'S LIBERATION

And the Woman sat on
    the curve
And cried: "I am only a woman!"
    "I am defenseless and can do nothing!!"
    "How unfortunate I am to be a woman!"
And she drowned in her own
    tears and self-pity.

And they found her body
    when the lake of tears dried up
And they said "The poor thing drowned . . .
    there was no way. . . . . . ."
And kept on walking nodding their heads.

And the Woman sat on
    the curve.
And says: "Damn concrete curve, how it penetrates!!"
    She got up and walked on,
    . . . stumbled on a stone . . .
And says: "Damn stone, it bruised my toe!!"
    Cursing she continued on and
    she bumped into a lampost. . . .
And says: "Damn lampost . . . what a great deal of pain it left
    me with!!!"

    BUT. . . . .
She went on and went on. . . . . . .
Arrived at her house. . . . . . .
And began making tortillas and Revolution.

Today I thought I'd call home
    so I got on the
        telephone
and said: "Operator please give me
    AZTLAN person to person"
She replied: "Sorry sir, still checking"
    after 2 minutes—
        She asked me to spell it—
So I did—
        A-Z-T-L-A-N
She thought I said ICELAND
at first but after the spelling she said
What?!!
        AZTLAN!
    She said is this some
    kind of a joke
        I said, "No, you
        know where it is"
    She said—"Sir I cannot
    take this call
But if you wish I'll
    let you talk to
my supervisor—"
        I said: "Fine
          Put 'em on
    I got time"—
Well her supervisor got on the line—
    And I told her what
I had said before
    All she could say was that
    was the first time she ever heard
    about it—I said, "You'll hear more
about it soon!"—and hung up—

                —*Carlos Cumpian*

CONTRIBUTORS

ABELARDO ("$") was born in Boquilla de Conchos, Chihuahua, México, in 1931, and came to the United States at the age of twelve. Currently employed as a Researcher for the Colorado Migrant Council in Denver, he is also editor of *The Farmworker's Journal*, editor-at-large for *La Luz* Magazine, and a prolific writer of fiction and nonfiction as well as of poetry. In 1977 he was awarded the Tonatiuh International Prize in Literature for two categories: short stories/poetry, and interracial books for children. "Poetry," he says, "has been a part of my life like one-a-day vitamins. . . . [It] inspires others, it serves as a chronicle where newspapers fail us and attacks with sharp wit our oppressors. In a personal matter it serves as an outlet which prevents insanity."

LEONARD ADAME ("Canto Pa' Mis Amiguitos") teaches for the Poetry in the Schools program in Fresno, California, where he was born in 1947, and will soon be attending the University of California at Irvine's Writing Workshop on a fellowship. His work has appeared in *The American Poetry Review, The Greenfield Review,* and several anthologies. His *Cantos Pa' la Memoria* has been published by Mango Press in San José as part of the Chicano Chapbook Series edited by Gary Soto. He began writing "because I had feelings that needed to be expressed," and he describes poetry as "the receptacle of many of my life experiences, which are, of artistic necessity, then refined and/or distilled into meaningful and cogent poems that, in turn, stand as completed entities."

ALURISTA ("nuestro barrio," "en el barrio," "must be the season of the witch," "ya estufas"), born in Mexico City in 1947, came to this country in 1961. He is presently completing his doctorate in Latin American Literature at the University of California in San Diego, where he teaches Chicano, Latin American, and Pre-Columbian Literature, Culture, and Thought. A prolific writer, editor, and lecturer, he is represented in every major anthology of Chicano literature and received the California Arts Council Creative Writing

Award for 1978. His books include *Floricanto en Aztlán, Nationchild Plumaroja, Tula y Tonau, Timespace Huracán, A'nque,* and *Spick in Glyph?*

RUDOLFO A. ANAYA (*Heart of Aztlán*) won the Second Annual Premio Quinto Sol for his first novel, *Bless Me, Ultima.* His third, *Tortuga,* is published by Editorial Justa in Berkeley, California. Currently he teaches Creative Writing at the University of New Mexico in Albuquerque.

HECTOR ANGULO ("Dopefiends Trip") lives in Los Angeles, the city of his birth; he is a printer and an artist as well as a poet, and his works have appeared in *Caracol* and in *Joint Conferences.* Here is how poetry entered his life and continues to influence it:

> Locked down
>   in a state prison cell
> my poetry came into being
>   a method
>   to penetrate the walls of confinement
> words formed
>   to communicate
>   feelings. . . . .
> for them living in a world
>   miles & miles apart
>   from my lifestyle
> and they (the people I corresponded with) responded
>   with their understanding
>   that said to me:
> they too have poetry in their hearts
>   so for real
>   when it comes from within
> now—in my freedom—I continue to write
>   because the need is there. . . . .

IVAN ARGUELLES ("The Spanish Girls") was conceived in Mexico, born in Minnesota (in 1939), and raised in Mexico City, Mexicali, Los Angeles, and then in Minnesota again. He is now a professional librarian for the University of California at Berkeley. His publications include two books of poetry—*Instamatic Reconditioning* and *The Invention of Spain*—and appearances in numerous journals and anthologies. He has been writing poetry for over twelve years: "The more I do it the more I am addicted to it. I am influenced by so many people and currents. . . . I love writing because it's the best way I know of to continue Dreaming." His influences reflect a wide and eclectic background: Joyce, Pound, Lorca, Dada, Surrealism, Dante, Virgil, the Sanskrit epics, modern Mexican poetry, Paz, Vallejo, Breton, Dino Campana, Murilo Mendes, Plato, Neo-Platonists, Sufi, the Hindu Bhakti school, and the T'ang Chinese.

SALOMON R. BALDENEGRO, JR. ("Man, I Felt Like Running All Night") was born in Douglas, Arizona, in 1944. He now lives in Tucson where he is Executive Director of Youth Development, Incorporated, and is involved in Chicano community activities. He began writing poetry fifteen years ago "as a means of expressing feelings and thoughts that I found difficult to articulate verbally. I thoroughly enjoy poetry and continue writing it because of the freedom it allows—i.e., one is able to express concepts, ideas, feelings, etc. without being tied down to conventions."

REYES CARDENAS ("Lowriders #2"), a native of Seguin, Texas, has written two novels: *Los Pachucos and la Flying Saucer,* and *Don Juan of the Snails.* His works have appeared in *Citybender, Dale Gas, Travois, Wood Ibis, El Grito,* and *Caracol.*

LORNA DEE CERVANTES ("Beneath the Shadow of the Freeway," "Visions of Mexico While at a Writing Symposium in Port Townsend, Washington"), born in San Francisco in 1954, is the founding editor, publisher, and printer of Mango Publications in San José. In 1978 she received a National Endowment for the Arts Creative Writing Fellowship grant, and was a Hudson D. Walker Fellow at the Fine Arts Work Center in Provincetown, Massachusetts, in 1979-80. Her works have appeared in several anthologies and magazines, among them the *Pushcart Prize, IV: Best of the Small Presses, The Third Woman, Década, Canto al Pueblo,* the *Latin American Literary Review, Grito del Sol, Caracol, Tin-Tan, Fuego de Aztlán,* and *Samisdat;* soon to be published by the University of Pittsburgh Press is a book of her poetry, *Emplumada.* She began writing at the age of eight: "I hated school, but on the sly I read everything that even faintly resembled a poem. This led me to Langston Hughes, Gwendolyn Brooks, and the world and wealth of Black literature in the sixties." After becoming a political activist, she "wanted to contribute something, to have some specific task or chore to carry out for the Movement, so when I discovered Chicano literature I realized that this was my natural role. I began bringing my work into the open and studying so that I could articulate clearly on paper. What began as a private emotional catalyst became a lifelong commitment." Now, she thinks of herself as a political writer whose awareness "came about through understanding the abstractions, such as 'race,' 'sex,' and 'class,' on a very personal level; I could connect the abstractions with all the corresponding intimate details of a life. This is what I would like my poems to do: to present the particulars, because there are no easy answers—only choices; and the ability to choose freely can sometimes be one's only true survival tactic."

CARLOS CUMPIAN ("Cuento") was born in San Antonio, Texas, in 1953, "the Year of the Snake." Presently in Chicago, he is a full-time student, works in a library, and is co-editor of the magazine *Abrazo*. He is working on a book of poetry and has been published in *The Spoon River Quarterly*, *Revista Chicano-Riqueña*, *Caracol*, the *Bayan Press Anthology*, and several local barrio newspapers. Writing "to keep myself from going out and crazy on the B.S. that is sweeping the pinche old planet," he also believes "it is the least I can do to begin to aid others en el movimiento toward self-determination. . . . The continuance of this poetic 'habit' will go on until I meet Victor Jara and some other very familiar cultural warriors I have known on this side of the universe. In time I'll turn to doing posters and hand-flyers for bus riders, paint words into wall murals and go skywriting."

NEPHTALI DE LEON ("In the Plaza We Walk"), currently living in Salt Lake City and working with SER, was born in Laredo, Texas, and raised around farm labor camps. In the 1960s he founded a newspaper, *La Voz de los Llanos*, in Lubbock, and has published numerous books of short stories, poems, and plays. Two of his books for children, *I Will Catch the Sun* and *I Color My Garden*, have been adopted for classroom use in California; his other publications include *Chicanos: Our Background and Our Pride*, *Chicano Poet*, *5 Plays*,

Coca Cola Dream, Hey, Mr. President, Man, Poems with Illustrated Woodcuts by Nephtalí, and *Tequila Mockingbird*.

RICARDO GONSALVES ("and") majored in Political Science at the University of California's San Diego campus. He now works in community affairs in the San Diego area.

JOSE ANGEL GUTIERREZ ("22 Miles"), a judge for the County of Zavala in Crystal City, Texas, was born in that city in 1944. He has been published in the *Texas Observer*, *La Raza* Magazine, *Nuestro*, *Caminos*, and several anthologies. Poetry, for him, is "a beautiful literary art form. Unlike public speaking and usual rhetoric, [it] has motion and romance." More important, it is "fun to write, relaxing to read and delicious to imagine."

JOSE MONTOYA ("La Jefita," "El Louie") was born in Escaboza, New Mexico, in 1932 and teaches art at California State University in Sacramento. His work has appeared in *Calafia, Giant-Talk, A Mark in Time*, and several other anthologies. In 1977 he received a California Arts Council Grant, and in 1979 a Writer's Fellowship at CSU Sacramento. For him, writing poetry "fulfills a need—and it keeps me from going under—and it makes me feel good to be contributing toward building a whole new and exciting body of knowledge— the world view of the Chicano!"

ALEJANDRO MURGUIA ("O California," "Small Towns"), born in 1949, came to the United States from Mexico City in 1956. Now a resident of San Francisco, he was awarded the 1980 Editor's Fellowship by the Coordinating Council of Literary Magazines for his work on *Tin-Tan*, and has published two books: *Oración a la Mano Poderosa* (poems) and *Farewell to the Coast* (short stories). His works have also appeared in the *Yardbird Reader, Tin-Tan, Revista Chicano-Riqueña, Hispanamérica, The California Bicentennial Anthology*, and *Calafia*. He defines poetry as the "ancient oral chant transmitted atavistic like by Nezahualcoyotl, Homer, Li-Po, Vatzayana, John the Baptist, Rimbaud, Isadore Ducasse, Otto René Castillo, Roque Dalton and Leonel Rugama who fired bursts of machine gun verse to liberate the children. We can only follow the trail to where the sun rises."

119

MARGARITA BALDENEGRO REYES ("The Old Man Who Is Gone Now") was born in 1942 in Douglas, Arizona, and now lives in Lawndale, California, with her husband and two children. She is a para-professional counselor at El Camino College and has completed requirements for a degree in Psychology at California State University's Dominguez Hills campus. Poetry, she says, is "my release valve. It keeps me balanced, mas o menos. I began writing out of anger. I'd fume in my head until, like the birth of Athena, a complete poem would emerge." Lately she has been writing short stories which she envisions as parts of a longer work.

MARINA RIVERA ("The Man of O"), born in 1942 in Superior, Arizona, teaches composition and literature to advanced high school students in Tucson; in the coming year she will be on sabbatical leave, working on a Master of Fine Arts degree. Her collected poems have been published in three chapbooks—*Mestiza, Sobra,* and *Concha*—and her works have appeared in several anthologies. She began writing poetry because "I was hungry. I felt ill," and continues to do so because "sometimes it's food, sometimes medicine. . . ."

TOMAS RIVERA ("M'ijo No Mira Nada") is Chancellor of the University of California at Riverside and for years has been active in the spheres of literature and higher education. Born in Crystal City, Texas, in 1935, he received his Ph.D. in Romance Languages and Literature from the University of Oklahoma, and came to UC Riverside from the University of Texas at El Paso. His publications include *Y no se lo tragó la tierra/The Earth Did Not Part, Always and Other Poems,* and numerous articles, monographs, and reports. He writes poetry because it "places me in contact with the original elements of life—good, evil, love, hate," and became involved with it "because of the need to be in touch with these original elements."

ALEIDA RODRIGUEZ ("Exploraciones/Bronchitis: The Rosario Beach House") came to the United States in 1962 from la Habana, Cuba, where she was born in 1953. She earns a living by "writing, editing, proofreading, pasteup, layout, publications coordination— just about anything in the publications field anyone is willing to pay me for." Her poems and short stories have been published in *Who's Who in Poetry in American Colleges and Universities, Momentum*

Magazine, New Magazine, Bachy 14, Pigiron Magazine, De Colores, Chrysalis 9, Beyond Baroque 802, L.A. Weekly, and *rara avis.* Describing the process that led to the poem which represents her in this anthology, she begins by noting that "when I start surfacing from one of the low periods [of not being able to write], I usually bring up material which is difficult for me—by that I mean new, and hard to find where the handle is. The Exploraciones series (of which "Bronchitis: The Rosario Beach House" is the second part) was one that followed such a dark period, and with it brought up my first language, Spanish, in which I'd written only phrases in previous poems. And I discovered that Spanish contained my emotions while English held my mind." Combining the two languages "seemed to fit my particular experience well—I, too, am fragmented by language; half of myself (my memories, etc.) is in one language, while the other half (my cognitive self, my intellect) is in another. I had never before worked in this manner and it was hard for me, but it began to turn on some lights in my past which had been before only a dark landscape. It has led me to write a series in English ("Little Cuba Stories") about the house I lived in as a child, moving room by room and recording the events they evoke."

LUIS RODRIGUEZ ("Over There in East L.A.") migrated to the West Coast with his family from Texas, and has lived throughout the Los Angeles area: Watts, the San Fernando and San Gabriel Valleys, San Pedro, and East L.A. Besides writing, he has worked as a truck driver, pipefitter, machinist, mechanic, carpenter, construction worker, paper mill worker, oil worker, and steel drill operator. He has also danced professionally, painted murals, been in jail, run for political office, and has been active in youth, tenant, and union movements.

RICARDO SANCHEZ ("Recuerdo . . .") was born in El Paso, Texas, in 1941; since 1977 he has been Visiting Assistant Professor at the University of Utah, where he was awarded the Merriner S. Eccles Fellowship for 1980-81. His many publications include *Canto y Grito Mi Liberación, Los Cuarto, Obras, Mano a Mano, Hechizospells, Milhuas Blues y Gritos Norteños,* and *Amsterdam Cantos y poemas pistos.* He began writing "in order to find my own meaning and the beauty of my people," and continues to do so "in order to better understand the beauty of human diversity and to help create history, a history of humanization."

LORENZA CALVILLO SCHMIDT ("Heading for Eugene") is one of nine children; her parents were farmworkers and she was born in Selma, California, in 1943. She holds a degree from the University of California at Berkeley and teaching credentials from Fresno State University. Presently an Associate Dean of Students at the University of California's Irvine campus, she is Director of an undergraduate residence hall complex and is Student Affairs Affirmative Action Officer. Her poetry has been published in *El Grito, The Journal of Ethnic Studies, First Chicano Literary Prize, Irvine 1974/75, Revista Chicano-Riqueña, The Bilingual Review,* and *Words.*

VICTOR M. VALLE ("Comida") was born in Fullerton, California, in 1950 and grew up in nearby Canta Ranas (now Santa Fe Springs). A part-time instructor of Folklore and Mythology at California State University, Long Beach, he is also a California Arts Council artist in residence, and Director of the Los Angeles Latino Writers' Workshop. He has been published by *Tin-Tan, rara avis, Maize, ChismeArte,* and *New Magazine,* and has appeared in one other anthology, *Calafia.* Among his awards are the *Caracol* Poetry Prize in 1979, and the Translation Award for 1980 given by the Columbia University Translation Center. He has just received a scholarship from the Medill School of Journalism at Northwestern University; after completing his graduate work he plans to translate Paolo de Carvalho-Neto's *Mi tío Atahualpa,* publish his translations of José María Arguedas and a family cookbook over a hundred and fifty years old, and then take up a career as a newspaper or magazine editor somewhere in the Southwest.

TINO VILLANUEVA ("Pachuco Remembered," "Aquellos Vatos"), who was born in San Marcos, Texas, in 1941, was a furniture factory worker for three years, and later spent twenty-two months with the United States Army in the Panama Canal Zone. He received his Bachelor of Arts degree from Southwest Texas State University, his Master of Arts from the State University of New York at Buffalo, and is currently a Ph.D. candidate in Romance Languages at Boston University; he is on the Spanish faculty at Wellesley College. He is the author of *Hay Otra Voz Poems,* and editor of *Chicanos: Antología histórica y literaria* (Fondo de Cultura Económica, México). "The most important fact about poetry," he believes, is that "it makes manifest the efficacy of words, offering a powerful condensation of feeling and thought. It synthesizes an experience in the least amount of discourse. Through it both poet and reader live out an enumerated microcosm suggestive of the larger and more significant macrocosm." He began to write at the age of twenty-five, and continues to do so "out of a love of language and its evocative power. Beyond that, two forces, or first causes, move my writing: 1) the wish to exercise freedom of the imagination so as to compose into and otherwise re-enact in words the pleasure of a private experience; and 2) the desire to chronicle scenes and developments of historical relevance as they affect Humankind, my country, my ethos and the empirical self." Describing the first category as "poetry of aesthetic appreciation" and the second as "poetry of humanist affirmation," he concludes that "poetry is certainly too vast to harness within merely two systems of thought, two modes of poetic expression. My own conviction is that the artist must not be encumbered by censorship, but rather be encouraged to explore themes of every order from all realms of thought and experience. This includes the external world of beauty and that of private sensation and intuition. He must be allowed as well the free flow of ideas in the face of human degradation, that is, in times of social ignominy when Humankind is dishonored."

ACKNOWLEDGEMENTS

In all cases I have reproduced these poems exactly as they appear in the sources cited below; those not acknowledged appear here for the first time to the best of my knowledge.

"Comida." Copyright 1978 by Victor Manuel Valle. By permission of the author.

"My Mother Pieced Quilts." From *Festival de Flor y Canto: An Anthology of Chicano Literature*, edited by Alurista, *et al.* (Los Angeles: University of Southern California Press, 1976), p. 34. Copyright 1976 by El Centro Chicano, University of Southern California. Reprinted by permission of University of Southern California Press.

"La Jefita." From *Aztlán: An Anthology of Mexican American Literature*, edited by Luis Valdez and Stan Steiner (New York: Random House, 1972), pp. 266-68. Reprinted by permission of the author.

"Beneath the Shadow of the Freeway." From *The Third Woman: Minority Women Writers of the United States*, edited by Dexter Fisher (Dallas: Houghton Mifflin Company, 1980), pp. 378-81. First appeared in *Latin American Literary Review* (Spring-Summer 1977). Revised version reprinted by permission of the author.

"Exploraciones/Bronchitis: The Rosario Beach House." From *La Cosecha/ The Harvest: The Chicana Experience, De Colores* IV, 3 (1978), pp. 83-85. Reprinted by permission of the editor of *De Colores* and of the author.

"Recuerdo . . ." From *Canto y grito mi liberación* (Garden City, N.Y.: Anchor Press/Doubleday, 1973), p. 109. Copyright 1971-1973 by Ricardo Sánchez. Reprinted by permission of the author.

"Canto Pa' Mis Amiguitos." From *Revista Chicano-Riqueña*, Año 5, núm. 4 (otoño 1977), pp. 9-10. Copyright by Leonard Adame. Reprinted by permission of the editor of *Revista Chicano-Riqueña* and of the author.

"The Old Man Who Is Gone Now." Copyright by Margarita Baldenegro Reyes. By permission of the author.

"Lowriders #2." From *Caracol,* 2, 9 (Mayo 1976), p. 12. Reprinted by permission of the editor of *Caracol* and of the author.

"In the Plaza We Walk." From *Caracol,* 1, 10 (Junio 1975), p. 20. Reprinted by permission of the editor of *Caracol* and of the author.

"La Peluquería Del Maestro." From *Revista Chicano-Riqueña,* Año 2, núm. 1 (invierno 1974), p. 26. Reprinted by permission of the editor of *Revista Chicano-Riqueña.*

"nuestro barrio," "en el barrio." From *Floricanto* (Los Angeles: University of California Press, 1971), pp. 87 & 36. Reprinted by permission of the author.

"Pachuco Remembered." From *Hay Otra Voz Poems (1968-1971)* (New York: Editorial Mensaje, 1972), p. 40. Copyright 1972 by Tino Villanueva. Reprinted by permission of the author.

"El Louie." From *Aztlán: An Anthology of Mexican American Literature* (New York: Random House, 1972), pp. 333-37. Reprinted by permission of the author.

"Aquellos Vatos." From *Hay Otra Voz Poems (1968-1971)* (New York: Editorial Mensaje, 1972), p. 42. Copyright 1972 by Tino Villanueva. Reprinted by permission of the author.

"El Mono Loco." From *Caracol,* 2, 5 (Enero 1976), pp. 12-13. Reprinted by permission of the editor of *Caracol.*

"must be the season of the witch." From *Floricanto* (Los Angeles: University of California Press, 1971), p. 26. Reprinted by permission of the author.

"Dopefiends Trip." From *Caracol,* 3, 9 (Mayo 1977), p. 19. Reprinted by permission of the editor of *Caracol* and of the author.

"$." From *Festival de Flor y Canto: An Anthology of Chicano Literature* (Los Angeles: University of Southern California Press, 1976), p. 34. Copyright 1976 by El Centro Chicano, University of Southern California. Reprinted by permission of University of Southern California Press, the author, and Barrio Publications.

"22 Miles." From *We Are Chicanos: An Anthology of Mexican-American Literature,* edited by Philip D. Ortego (New York: Washington Square Press, 1973), pp. 212-15. Reprinted by permission of the author.

"M'ijo No Mira Nada." From *El Espejo-The Mirror: Selected Chicano Literature*, edited by Octavio Ignacio Romano-V. and Herminio Ríos-C. (Berkeley, California: Quinto Sol, 1972), p. 244. Copyright by Tomás Rivera. Reprinted by permission of the author.

"The Spanish Girls." From *Revista Chicano-Riqueña*, Año 4, núm. 2 (primavera 1976), pp. 38-39. Reprinted by permission of the editor of *Revista Chicano-Riqueña* and of the author.

"The Man of O." From *Revista Chicano-Riqueña*, Año 7, núm. 3 (verano 1979), pp. 22-23. Reprinted by permission of the editor of *Revista Chicano-Riqueña* and of the author.

"Visions of Mexico While at a Writing Symposium in Port Townsend, Washington." First published in *Mango*. Reprinted by permission of the author.

"O California." From *Festival de Flor y Canto: An Anthology of Chicano Literature* (Los Angeles: University of Southern California Press, 1976), p. 126. Copyright 1976 by Alejandro Murguía. Reprinted by permission of University of Southern California Press and of the author.

"Small Towns." Reprinted by permission of the author.

"Heading for Eugene." From *Revista Chicano-Riqueña*, Año 4, núm. 1 (invierno 1976), pp. 20-21. Reprinted by permission of the editor of *Revista Chicano-Riqueña* and of the author.

"Man, I Felt Like Running All Night." Copyright by Salomón R. Baldenegro, Jr. By permission of the author.

"ya estufas." From *Nationchild Plumaroja* (San Diego: Toltecas en Aztlán, 1972), unnumbered. Reprinted by permission of the author.

"and." From *Maize*, 1, 3 (primavera 1978), pp. 14-15. Reprinted by permission of the editor of *Maize*.

"Sobre la Liberación de la Mujer." From *Revista Chicano-Riqueña*, Año 3, núm. 2 (primavera 1975), pp. 9-10. Reprinted by permission of the editor of *Revista Chicano-Riqueña*.

"Cuento." From *Caracol*, 3, 9 (Mayo 1977), p. 21. Reprinted by permission of the editor of *Caracol* and of the author.

I would also like to thank the following writers for their excerpts which I have used to introduce the three sections of the book:

Robert Coles. *The Old Ones of New Mexico* (Anchor Books/Doubleday, 1975), pp. 76-77. Reprinted by permission of the author.

Luis Rodríguez. "Over There in East L.A." In *L.A. Weekly* I, 33 (July 20-26, 1979), p. 6. Copyright 1979 by Luis Rodríguez. Reprinted by permission of the author.

Rudolfo A. Anaya. *Heart of Aztlán* (Berkeley, California: Editorial Justa Publications, P.O. Box 2131-C), pp. 207-8. Copyright 1976 by Rudolfo A. Anaya. Reprinted by permission of the author.